Greek Sport

Contents

Written by Lindsay Galvin

Illustrated by Mike Phillips

Collins

Let the sports begin!

The torch is lit with a spark so the Greek Sports can begin. Stop preening that beard! Stoop and thank the gods.

Go under the arch to meet the crowd ...

Running

Did you train hard? You must sprint up and down a 192 m track at top speed.

Wait at the starting block. Do not go
too soon ...

The discus

The discus is a disk of rock. Bend at the waist and spin. Then let it zoom!

When you are waiting, stand clear!

Boxing

You spar with fists, but be smart – duck and scoot as well.

You cannot complain when you get hit ...

The javelin

The javelin is a long spear with a point. Grip the strap tight, run, aim well, then shoot it high and far.

Check the coast is clear. It is so sharp!

Horses

Perch on the cart and flick the straps
for speed.

Hang on tight – the horses are too quick to stop!

The winner

You are the winner – proof that you are the best at Greek sports!

Now claim the crown. Will it be silver or copper?

The crown is not silver or copper. It is twisted twigs from a tree!

The crowd claps and yells, so you are not disappointed.

Training then and now

The right food for lunch will help you in all the Greek sports.

You might be worn out, but do not
miss training! And do not be a clown or
groan, if you wish to get the winner's crown!

Can you spot the Greek sports on the jars?

horses   discus   boxing

21

Greek sports

Review: After reading

Use your assessment from hearing the children read to choose any GPCs, words or tricky words that need additional practice.

Read 1: Decoding

- Turn to page 11 and point to the word **coast**.
  - o Ask: What is a coast? (e.g. *a shoreline, land by the sea*)
  - o Encourage the children to read the whole sentence. Ask: What does **the coast is clear** mean? Point out how this phrase is used to mean you are free to do something because there's no danger nearby.
- Focus on words with long vowels and adjacent consonants. Ask the children to sound out and read:
  spar   scoot   smart   speed   sports   spear   complain
- Point to the headings on each left-hand page. Challenge the children to read them aloud fluently, sounding out in their heads silently if necessary.

Read 2: Prosody

- Ask the children to read pages 4 and 5 as if they are a trainer. Encourage them to emphasise words to clarify what they want their competitor to do and not do.
- Model reading page 4, emphasising, for example, **must** and **top speed**.
- Give the children time to experiment reading a page to a partner before taking turns to read to the group.

Read 3: Comprehension

- Ask the children if they have done any sports that are similar to the Greek sports. In what ways are they different/the same?
- Ask: Is this a story book or is it non-fiction? (*non-fiction*) Ask the children what they have learnt about ancient Greek sports. Ask: Does it show you what it feels like to do Greek sports?
- Focus on words that can have two meanings.
  - o Ask the children to think of synonyms, for these words:
    train   hard   scoot   duck
  - o Ask the children to find the original words on pages 4 and 8. If they replace the words with their synonyms, do the sentences still make sense?
  - o Discuss the children's findings.
- On pages 22 and 23, encourage children to identify each sport. What can they remember about it?
- Bonus content: Look at pages 18–19 together. Talk about the similarities and differences in training now and in ancient Greek times. Can children think of any other ways of training for sports?
- Bonus content: Discuss the pictures on the jars on pages 20–21, and talk about which might go with which label.